Kin

Russell Buker

Copyright © 2020 *Kin* by Russell Buker

Published by Piscataqua Press
an imprint of RiverRun Bookstore
32 Daniel Street
Portsmouth NH 03801

ISBN: 978-1-950381-65-4

Russell Buker recently retired from Shead High School where he taught English and Creative Writing. He has also coached for many years: football, baseball, basketball and tennis.

Russell has had numerous poems accepted in many publications in the U.S. and in Canada: *The Antigonish Review, The Windrow Anthology, The Cape Breton Collection, Pottersfield Press, Goose River Anthology, Portland Press Poetry Section, The Aurorean, Felt Sun, The Aputamkan Review*. Russell has also served on the board of editors and written book reviews for *Off the Coast Review*.

Contents

This book is dedicated to the memory of

Beth Allan

Kenneth Buker

my youngest sister and older brother who passed

in the early months of an unsettling 2020

Totality

pink flames emerge
how
will I restore the
real
pages something has
yet
to be known as I
follow
Caliban wandering the
streets
collapsing desires to
live
asking would you
like
to cut my hair, no
big
task with male pattern
baldness
or would you like to
see
my immunity passport
for
heaven as guerrilla
grafter
fruit onto sterile
city

trees body labor as

apple

for the homelessness

that

keeps us on the move

daily

while ignoring the broken

glass

dreams of everyone

Aporia

look carefully for
me
had not meant to
fall
asleep but our
hands
were interlocked
protecting
the space between
them
as to who we were
when
together when the space
expanded
between our bodies
let
no man put asunder
roared
in our small room
while
outside flowing tarmac
that
locks in our building
rose
in the sunlight on
waves

defying our gravity
of
its own making and
yet
somehow transporting
us
beyond our beginnings
so
we were left seeking
each
others hands once
again

Shekhinah at 80

Sorry to drag you into
this
again as I know you
suffer
with us that you live
among
and Dantean beasts always
block
our short way up

the only sky affordable
to
me brightens today
so
many days of inert and yet
some-
where this Covid 19
is
supposed to peak gnawing

nor
is there any joy watching
waiting
Raven pair as the returning
Robbins

dance their way into the
bare
spots of a slow, auspicious
spring

Free will

blindness
choice blindness
brain
creating reality

all that
time
spent in the dark
listening

to the sea's worn
grind
you might

remember me
now
that I don't
remember

receding
from
today's walk
in

the poem- park
unsure
if I was the one
diving

for shiny coins

in

the stagnant still

pool

with defunct shower

and

ripe fountain's

silt

Been

Royally ruined before
becoming
walking in this scary
night
testing to see what follows
three
steps stop listen
for
the soft footfall
that
hadn't anticipated
my
stopping and as ears
strain
I wait before resuming
if
it were my soul chances
are
it would have stopped
when
I did nor is there a moon
shadow
birth so on I walk stop
at
will thrilled with a
voice-
less accompaniment

Halloween at 80

I admit to stumbling
a little
out of breath too
finally
made it to my front
door
relatives, stars long
exhausted
tried tripping me
unsure
if I had ever lived up
to
mediocre frost killed
heritage
as my garden flowers
became
me after months of no
response
became the boundaries
felt
of my beliefs that I
knew
enough not to be too
sure
of even though frost
has
changed them too soon

because

I do know I am next to last

of

my families star light

chasing

me in this darkness

to

my unlocked front door

Dreaming of sleep

I attempt to fall
asleep
among empty bottles
discarded
food carriers along
aspirations
highway's cluttered
road
without a road sign
my
other world of loving
you
has become too narrow
what
with always almost
falling
maneuvering on crazy
feet
that seem to have
grown
another inner slab
soul
precariously between
sole
and ankle that causes
flailing

and lacking a Blues

mentality

can only imagine the

safety

of long grass at the

edge

of a long, long highway's

hum

of cars racing somewhere

Rumpled vision

another long day
relentless
fog with wisps
bouncing
along and I see
half
a woman walking
her
dog, a man without
hands
getting into his car
carrying
his coffee cup
wife
wants to know
if
I want breakfast
sorry
I say no teeth
where
are you anyway
am
soaked to the bone
will
wait for a sunny dry
day

When

I cease to remember
you
most evenings I
can
only face those
stars
alone in my vision
tell
them that here
in
my beloved mountains
have
known my share of
wind-
a prisoner so to
speak-
then they seem to
glow
a bit brighter
telling
me that celestial
storms
are not for mere
humans
to withstand and
when

my light does not
return
their shine it will be
gone
quickly extinguished by
a
failure that's submerged
in
synesthesia where
your
song's colored flowers
smell
of early springtime

Finale

finally over the
edge
not even remembering
the
remains hung on long
after
the proverbial bough
broke
emphasis on the un-
heard
snap written on the
morning's
dew of that beloved
train
station that waited
until
sun pawed through
dust
scribbled windows
way
above our feeling's hor-
izons
in the ebb and flow of
extinction

Melancholy fog

this fall weather's
capable
of shutting off
doctored
beams-more play
than
we could ever
want
till those slowing
steps
slack vision whets
our
appetite for self
inspection
deception what have
I
done to myself
all
these years and for
what
as I trusted my
compass
19 degrees East to
make
my way out of the
silken

harbor hearing other
boats
revving while I tactfully
avoid
buoys that come upon
me
as I make my way
out
to sea again

Then

the view never
changed
outside my grimy
hospital
window- wanted to sing
but
strings attached to
lungs
wouldn't move
as
I bounced up or
down
between living
and
the dead nights when
darkness
withdrew the image
slowly
from my gaze
only
relinquished by
slow
coming of light
that
the nurse said was
the first

time I had missed
through
sleep and that was
good
sign that you're
recovery's
coming while closing
curtains

Still

we can still be
dropped
yes
dropped from floating
note
there is no telling
where
we as infants
pushed
from the womb
nerves
loosened with nothing
to
lose as the note floated
away
leaving symphony playing
music

October 3rd

being almost there
again
birthdays strain
yet
no longer able to
give
my eye teeth
there
was nothing I could
do
but render everything
perfectly
in a wild attempt
to
keep the grass down
still
it rains a lot in these
parts
forcing us to walk
buoyant
grass keeping our
heads
up knowing we are
closer
than ever, never
again

Atman

nightly
I could not believe
different
pages of poems pass-
ing
through my REM
sleep
were so indecisive
close
to readability yet
never
legible- so much
for
laser surgery's 20/20
worse
unable to pin them as
mine
while they scrolled
just
fast enough to blur
well
why not adsorb some
for
morning coffee's swirls
non
sugared coherence hot

havens
seeking breath in the
mist

Today

seems to me as though
every
dream I've ever had
has
landed in my frozen
foot
topped off with sugars
from
starches and screwed
on
tightly to ward off
decay
meanwhile my mouth
moves
for about a year or
so
mouthing silent words
not
all sweet or harmonious
while
the rest of my body just
settles
and of course I see
nothing
no dew no sun battling
sand

Excarnation

upon death is there
more
than one soul departing
moral
purification like lichen
which
has so many disappear
to
somewhere plus join
mine
and everyone's in a
quiet
pool of deep thought

sad will I be if those
lichen
souls quibble over
allowing
me to enter as both
fungus
and alga are represented
while
I
am of single natures both
over-
whelmed by dry souls
needing
water desperately

Gifting

giving gas money
to
our families addict
thinking
he must have had a
rapacious
father to keep in-
serting
the word dad in his
stories
how clear in the
absence
of ailments I see
clearly
from his father's hell
as
we imagine a hawk
balanced
on a tree limb pecking
away
at a tonic rabbit who
calls
him sweet dad until
his
bones are cast from the
tree

toward the perfect

now

of luminosity

Voyageur

under this sun's
threat
this morning I
would
like to take my
canoe,
before freezing
skims
get serious, slowly
through
mists on the lake
say
hello missed you
all
these years startled
where
stout maples have
grown
more, finally blown
down
loom over water's
edge
where alert fish
call
for lowering snag-
like
providing mirror nests

now
trepidation as my
boat
reels upon maples
mist
I am in water above
water
now must paddle
through
branches hanging in
air
to visit the lonely
loon
somewhere out there

Jere

Be safe my friend as
rain
drives down our
green
fears and prayers
playing
about our feet
before
noisy wind lifts
them
past clenched teeth
and
mouth opened just
enough
to quarter breath
escaping
involuntarily heading
beyond
the visible roar of
branches
roof shingles and any-
thing
in the yard not picked
up

Sicarius

I have grown so old
and
I can not breathe
man
those leaves this year
will
not shrink at all nor
litter
their root's ground so
how
could one Sicari,
Wednesday,
man be ordered to
ruin
so much for everyone
to
placate those who empow-
ered
his star less nights where
30
pieces stretch longer
than
those silver songs of
youth
where choking begins
another
sunless Saharan day

Poets are primed to fall

no one likes to
fall
especially in late
summer's
crusty rind lessoned
from
within while blues
raged
in warm days
I
curdled against my
tilting
yet some mechanism
prompted
me rise as even
fearful
pups howl into full
flooding
moon where an owls
who
wants to know about
moon's
liquid demise and how
I got
so dirty with only a
plastic

skin imprisonment

before

final vanishing

Perhaps

why I chose- suspicious
limp-
in the light air yesterday
brought
perhaps I should have
worked
harder- birds have flown
again
and will today too
most
of the outside dancers
have
returned home some
wetter
than others and just
as
I learned to talk on
paper
my tongue began to
split
my side versus wish-
full
thinking on biting
on
bleeding you again
for
your retort-perhaps

Gaul

Heavy footprints
bent sword
killed in warrior
death
accompany him
where-
ever a muddled
word
takes him after
living
in cacophonous
battle
needed but a grunt
or
two until exhausted
men
made certain those
lying
there were all
dead
and the bending
of
swords began in
earnest

Skirmish

85 degrees and
humid
we are clouded
today
like these pota-
toes
many blind eyes
watch
Gaia-Enceladus
galaxy
already consumed
with
red-blue halo's
blood
brain barrier
liquify
the soil beneath
our
dining room table
crust
uneasy here also
wonder
why I have been
kept
foolish this crab en-
croaching
foreign pool rotation

during
a minor earth-quake
shake

3rd face

chance is without
memory
I withdraw my
hand
but they- memories
long
awake begin again
warm
my hand which
does
not remember what
frequency
to turn on which
one
to want, worse
how
did I get here
my
sister Elaine flew
off
on a sky-blue linen
one
knob turned correctly
I swear
she thinks she can
fly
with hers anywhere

while

I mumble in my

lament

Would

would we know where

when

or what would we be

without

water or when there

is

no longer a web of

life

but a true vertigo

where

I'm always falling

from

ladders propped

every

where imaginary walls

heave

oceanic-ally pretending

fall

hydration inundating

deserts,

mountains one last

time

before begone before be

born

before kisses move

us

hurry on this sky

reddens

Katabasis

first I remember wheeled
wood
cutters as they had
given
all of our trees
then
mighty bulldozers
came
pushing the landscape
ahead
so that our skyline
could
be interrupted which
matters
as now no one's allowed
on
their property with
rugged
poles and steel sky-
scrapers
choppers will come
spurring
orange on small trees
and
we pray no ice/any
storms
will devastate this
for

we will be billed

extra

 to pay for mayhem

and

those recipients will

grumble

at interruptions of

service

look for alternative

sources

80

who did I think

I

was moon in

trees

flitting poem to poem

in

a place I hoped to

belong

but never hastened

to

those trees cringing

unable

to flee- how does

one

celebrate this 80

thing

when tree battered

winds

youth that steered

colors

of blue in reflective

night

certain I would

release

any anchors developed

in

vain to my favorite

ghost
garden's clouded
cataracts
with every unused
DNA
kept in a high density
area
with a folding pattern
within
a pattern called my
fractal
globule's informational
paradox
May's Blue Moon's
back
in those trees again
Ah
to be 79 again

Where

I am but four
thoughts
again towards
self
preservation
if
I preserved my
work-
noise made in the
night
by a prey animal
un
heeded as a
monster-
with
sinking heart syn-
drome
who casts about to
see
if they are finally
watching
those pages fly and
bare
bones left for
heat
of the brilliant
rays

every long day
tourists
questioning ab-
stractly
who was that

Picture

what latent energy
is
it that reflects my
body
at its elemental
edges
that wants me to
call
out in a lost star
language
to enable me to
pass
on frozen reactions
under-
standing how I had
tumbled
so far away for
so
long until falling
into
this thing I call
me

He sweet danced

down
main street
hey
dingle do
water
sings yessir it
do
people like
me
change their
odor
when wet
stink
driving to doctor's
waiting
room where
ladies
pilfer magazines
I
have brought and
they
have stopped
buying
of special teas
vacations
to exotica to
rejuvenate

Christe
I'm going to
call
an Uber and
drive
dangerously
home

Now

don't be too hasty
I tell
the undertakers assistant
who
is about to shove a
piece
of plastic up my ass
to keep
my gut from flatulent
moans
listen I say words are
spiritual
few will listen anyway
the rest
will be hiding their own
symptoms
and you who tampered
with
my own DNA afraid I
was
to be an anomaly
why
not I don't mind being
a dead
end twig on the family
tree

or hideous bloom soon
to die
with a hunk of plastic
stuck
up my farty ass

I really did not have
anywhere to run

heat lightening flashes
cat
anticipates thunder
that
will make its way
here
tonight just as we
are
moving out from
under
our thatched roof
that
resembles morning
sky
whose heart seems
weighted
down with its lisp
of
trembling faintness our
vestibule
of calm wanting
waiting
for the sun to dry the
the memories memorized
in
water hydrated in me

Inevitability

we have been sitting
by our
doorway watching
those
walkers walking
walkers

oh I've fallen
hear
that small cry
help

my video camera
shakes
in unsteady hands
falls

my god it's
position
that makes me
exotic

the old trick
hand
to elbow elbow to
hand

videos cut on
cutting
room cluttered floors
Gypsies
curling at our feet

I will pick you
up
my eyes voice
within

Helium Hydride

I was certain
that
I had swept
all
words into the
dust
bin of sleep
when
helium Hydride
floated
by my eyes
shining
alone for so
long

as with so
many
Dr's visits
Andromeda
beckons
ahead of Lani-
kea
that great attractor
without
compassion
without
dogmatism

draws

knowing all

combo's

do not work

out

and I am

one

destined

for the loneliness

of

Spartan Woods

among

the childish prattle

of

autumn leavings

relatives

moving or desiring

to

do so before snow

Happening as happenstance

X squared x Y squared = 1
cheeks already
dark
minstrel man
feet
traveling boards
in
big, dark fields
circleing
big, dark trees
rung
round with dis-
ease
smiling breathlessly
this
is great comedy
slap
struck through
life
X squared x Y squared =circle
peeled
from mirror to
mirror

Re entry

unique as the how's of
sanity
when our/my universe
has
gone from singularity
to
singularity prior to
exploding
again
towards another re-
menbrance
wishing for some reason
hope
that there will be
remnants
of our serene floating
around
in clouds of Wordsworthian
glory
or become a point again
pointless
waiting statistically
comfort-
able as non significant
ergo
as shadows follow a
child
standing on one foot

Back

stand
something special
but
no longer an impulse
yet
still braving myself
into
the darkest of this
night
where the conscious
words
lie tangled, feeling for
ones
to extract slowly
amassing
as we all slide
back
back into the times
before
that big bang inter-
rupted
snowfalls of bending
regret
borrowed words
worlds
that stand apart worlds
apart

bodily pain strewn
our
only light
light

Raven

single black
Raven
longing for
break-
fast and a
hello
whatever the
weather
I greet you
dream
scape
like always now
though
you no longer
see
me busting
snow
off the truck
as
though this
much
camouflage
was
way too much
reminding
you preferred
that

aluminum
heating
plate to the
cheap
pastry leftover

Stupid

dreams last
night
does it matter
where
my final dust's
laid

learning to
love
again- past
erections
time-you
so
long ago

playing with
our
newness under
water
unseen and
careful

careful youthful
Sherpa's
crossing a crevasse
studded
boots meant
for ice

on an unsequered
aluminum
ladder on one
end
my end to be
sure

now we swim
away
from under the
raft
red faced like
break
and enter thieves

hoping
to not have been
seen
by everyone
who
knows what's
up

with us and

Rosa

Rugosa's along

the

sand beaches per-

imeter

Tribute to Dean Kostos

In a dry world more huge than rhyme or dreaming
We hear the sentences of straws and stones,
Stand in the wind and, bowing to this time,
Richard Wilbur

A liquid kaleido
scope
appears where the
sentence
lies on the page
of
my father's notebook

walking through the Louvre
pictures
sing peasant songs and
I
can not bring myself
to
leave till the song's
over

it was me always
listening
to mother's red anger
behind
closed doors that

they
ascertained orange
yellow
lime I was mad as

I
always turned apple
core
white while her
body's
nerves frost white
stabbed
bubbly pink feet

and
of course my black
voice
yelling at whoever
was
sneaking into my
room
when I was gone

give him time to
blue
on out of there cloud
white

How

sun-
shine way past the
apex
of my learning
curve
almost back to
zero
I stand where I
should
feel the strength
of
sun on my un-
clothed
body's imperfect garden

how many years with
out
sunshine blocked by
those
extended lies of their
tv,
social computers phoned
into
hands holding manipulating
platitudes
dreamed this day would

come
with my voice un
heard

wondering if my garden
ever
flowers and if that
returning
tv signal sent out
into
space so long ago
will
pick up enough
energy
to document this crisp
silence

Kvakeri

This is just a scrap
she
motioned to an old
window
on her living room
wall
irrelevance No,no
its
got to be translated
as
colonized life story
slippage
and slow disappearance
of
what we love of here and
now
much like those Russian
sub
mariners at max depth
listening
as something came
upon
them at greater speed
known
and whooshed by them
dehumanizing
them as the sound pattern

emerges
then the faltering words
ahaded
into its probable meaning

Bright mothers, bright fathers

they often huddled wondering
what
to do with me and so I
worried
where would be the best
place
to pass my flesh less
bones
in hopeful dryness to
future
generations patrichor on the
floor
and why did I think some-
one
would come along wonder-
ing
what kind of beast was this
and
why did he spend so much
time
on a disastrous writing
career
like the time I bought nuts
to
feed the cities pigeons
and
they swarmed me landing

on

my shoulders and my silly

comb

over exposing my decrepit

deception

so that I threw the whole bag

as

far away as I could to let

them

fight over it while I walked

away

stepping over a dead pigeon

not

knowing how much good

he

had wrought or what would

happen

to his stiffening carcass's

marks

of weakness, marks of woe

that

continue since Blake's time

we

now are full of fear, anxious

about

where and when that certain

woman

and her three bears will no
longer
protect our carrying on as
though
we are certain of what we
are
doing with all those children
with
all those children's commodities
frozen
in time for future use of parts
plasma
or virginal screams, sore
bleeding
at the hands of rapacious
ineptitude

New Year's Day 2020

Disappointment I
know
you are lurking
always
on the night of the
long
est thunders-least
expected-
how you laugh
chortle
egg me on for a
go
with another flash
to
cry out and hoot
then
spills moon-like
while
I tried consoling these
trees
holy tabernac al-
most
reaching my toes as
I
live and breathe knowing
life
has decorated more

time
finding facts in the
water's
of the world and these
material
words would have au-
stounded
ancestors who did
similar
things but could not
utter
any directions

Hmm

another near death
but
she said shortly
sugar
it was probably
blood
pressure not
famished
ghosts streaming
around
my room that
night
but I knew my
hand
was held and
I
turned myself
completely
around twice before
losing
consciousness as
when
swimming too far
from
an unseen shore
those
strengthening waves

began

toying with me

and

all I could do

was

hold my breath

till

I felt someone's

hand

reach from a boat

pull

me aboard gently

silently

in a yellow Sou-

wester

and

we took turns rowing

home

Dreams of long

I in my red-checked
hunter's
plaid the cart is
mesh
bag on four wheels

those free trees
have
shattered greed
grabbed
every shaft of light

with
wide leaves on
this
warm avenue of
pound

to the swishing
fountain
of pure nightfall
intent

too old to care
about
death- let it be
silent
thicket solitary

while
the nightingales
long
song calls the night
for

respite proof that
song
is enough while
still
reverberating

Starting sterile

I wanted to tell
you
I who have been
so
far away of late
with
borrowed paper
want
to tell you, everyone
how
far away the mind
can
exit in any direction
away
from free will
before
looping back to me
you:
the brilliant light
slowing,
the extreme cold
holding
awful sky- boy- blue
vision
of me static it's
nothing

I knew I'd be
awe-
some wind stalling
any
thought of freedom
way
before stern question
where
did you toss my
pants
OK, what's for break-
fast

Reading my thoughts

Being on this
side
of the window
has
taken its toll

I dream of you
mornings
early mornings
way
before the dangerous

sun
flecks through my
images
you fly into the
window

between us thinking
you
know the harmony
that
is us, was us and
all

I can do now
is

pick you up
hold
you or leave you

for
the feral cat
gracious
that will also want to
come

in with feathers
stuck
to his thin chin
purrs
for my lap

Girolamo Savonarola

Where in galaxy

heaven

I wondering, wandering

why

for what reason

was

I screaming in

night-

fear of bonfire

we

wake to our alarm

is

this my own

of

the vanities as I

was

moving- not from

or

to Florence- but

all

favorite class or

bought

were burning, roaring:

strong

words left first be-

tween

fire and smoke

snapping
in freedom-down
hill
fun is so brief
then
it was another
flame
all twenty-two of
mine
from strife, dreams
bent
over in debilitating
repose
old foot-falls thud
slowly
nigh times are
rough

Blank face

quorum response
dreams
are not yours to
save
your heredity is
stored
family tree re-
duced
comfort in knowing
error
is part of us as
single
trees standing alone
in
a landscape always
stir
in us a reason for
fort-
titude inspite of the
season
we have grown used
to
with the immediate
let-
down after said
response

Branch

more sunlight than
we've
seen in a while
I
squint at workers
cleaning
remnants of branches
broken
in age, losing conflict
with-
out so much as a leaf
left
were I still part of a
family
tree with long history
but
not much variegating as
these
branches were never
straight
selfish leaves curled
unto
themselves with coughing
virus
shaking and no one
would
help- too old to waste

our

time and meds on

so

there only another

generation

of quaking branches

higher

up there see it already

softens

then this tree will be done

for

Waste

when La Di Dah
makes
its final appearance
time
has wasted your time
you
wasted on of all things
so
painted on those empty
pages
as tears, not in pity
but
assimilation, my
sleep
has sent yes you, yes
me
and those pearly Ravens
lead
me to where the wet
lane
subducts the drier tar
mac
so near the end again
that's
so urban, urbane no
urban

Another Dream

It is when I am sick
again
fear exchanging for
more
and afterglow light has
brought
brain signals here
sifting
through this hologram
that
I can now dictate my self
like
Einstein's spooky action
formed
along in this other universe
dictate
or will myself there, no
need
of propulsion, and assume
my-
self there beginning
again
now I'm anything I
imagine
light stays on unlike
those
days of myriad black
holes

Oumuamua

aroused by our heavy-
ness
I can tell by the noise
hope's
no longer a bright
globe
You point a finger-
tip
at our complacency's
bounded
space
in spite of our being
struck
before killing Arctic
forests
ponderous animals and
those
would-be birds had
they
learned to escape our
delicious
gravity that you willingly
seek
but secretly whoosh
by
welcome Oumuamua from
afar

welcome to our refreshing
tides

Ken

from the last room

you

were in may you

now

thank our parents

inter-

twined, woven, early absence

warp

of your own transcontinental

journal

woof from dad's loom and

now

if at all possible sing

to

them the possibility of

those

root-beer bottles exploding

again

in the cellar of our potent

dreams

Ornaments

leaves on the earth's
land
slip we stoically stalk
feet
scrambling on disappearing
darkening
crust with one question
why
who did this to us
this
certainty of plague-
like
narrowing of our gene
pool
to what end urinator in hand
as
rivers gush, trees crash
with
their stored sunlight. Thorny
brambles
all we have to hold onto
what
should be our response
keeping
in mind that we can man-
ipulate
a toy on Mars from a

tiny

room in our home here

yet

have not learned to

govern

or why we should

I'm

smiling
to myself watching
our
neighbors
paper being delivered
by
a bald man without a
bicycle
as it is being delivered
in a
van- maybe the bike's
inside
the van with a cotton
paper
carrier- maybe the hills and
puddles
do not matter as the news
has
changed too according to
the owner's
politics and nowhere is
all
the news that is fit to
print
delivered to your round
box
with the premise of
keeping

it dry anyway my neighbor
took it
went right to the comic page
cross
word with its request for a
jumble
of language poetry's wordy
intelligence
signifying time well spent

Prescription

ranting cant,can
not
danger plus change

living
in a strange room
now

I should be anything
I
imagine freedom

being
just nameless
energy

wondering if I'm
really
with you now

blood
on the snow or
your

blouse means we're
obliged
to look at those

vibrations
of undefinable
color

that holds the void
inside
itself childlike

and
the last to know
fear

OK

who owns my
past
the past who
stands

there observant
claiming
mine all mine

that
was a year ago
before
I donated more

and
gave it to whom-
ever

is up there still
grasping
keeping my head
up

looking for more
that's
the predictable game

we
are forced to play
today
wondering if we did

OK
hey, hey till we
run

out of falsetto
futures
then what, what

Damnatio Memoriae

this is a shallow,warm

sea

to waddle in and

now

that my body's

not

the only place to

live

in where should I

begin

to set myself adrift

as

I too distraught

hydrogen

arcing around stars winking

helium

close to my wind-burned

memory

of animals, trees list-

ening

to tight drums of friends

who

along with Diogenes

Goethe

knew the light's value

that

awakened all receptors

of
my eyes in the small
hidden
aquarium of my soul

Mt Blue

have to admit this
was
a hard climb at sixty
five

what's so amazing
is
I could not feel my
self

attached to this to earth
or
the time it took to get
here

where I stood shadow
less
on my mountain in
silence

clouds came with
out
noise prodigiously
past

what I remembered
to be

me with opened
mouth

clouds rushed past
quiet
teeth joining the
air

that entered nostrils
so
that I felt levitated
peer

on the other side
where
even my hands were
quiet

Traces

there are days
when
I willingly take
all
my meds succumbed
engulfed
by promises to keep
me
alive and then there are
days
when I relish left
over
Pizza for breakfast
giddy
with freedom of sub-
jucation
of mere voyeurism
wild
eyed at not knowing
when
I'll stop being their
consumer
dodge the headstones
on
my own for a while
among
the frowns of cloudy
skies

Impact

Let the failing light
curl and cuddle the
emergent maples

and cooling air
from lower fields
come seeking me

I find myself missing
my daughter lately she
endured my silence

yet would exclaim
to no one " I'm cold "
and we would go on

in her telling me that
inevitably the light
fails even up here

Salvage

old Merc is going
retro-
grade, seemingly, again
apparently
why I feel so confused
only
able to reflect on my
past's
high intuition rates
I'm
the one who stumbles
in
the woods while forest
bathing
bordering on coincidences
and
the sad silence of rejection
with-
out an erection to tear
down
to repaint in my own
image
as I salvage what is
good
dust in the balance yes
dust
my new/old history on the
ground

Drought

the light of all the
not
yet stars drifting
a
bright mist... Rebecca Elson

everything has receded
lawn
makes strange noises
as
though an early frost
when
you walk on it

rivers
and lakes have shrunk
as
have words that have
taken
on a different hue
smiles

belch bile in this
coarse
city of blaming every-
one

suspect while old sores
scarred
over begin to bleed

new governing bodies
shoot
dissenters who wont get
serious
while Christ is pulled
off
church walls to rest

no one noticed the
solstice
has come and gone
with
shortening daylight
thrill
of power beckons

Good by

Robert Frost stood
among
his mutually rooted
trees
and said good by

by
and keep cold-like-
wise
I have been dreaming
walking

barefoot on the lawn
feeding
Ravens left-over
cat
food while neuropathy

wants more morning bent
grass
blasting star like energy
posted
on face book's page

until
I no longer see myself
nor

can anyone feel the sparks
breath

I felt as Mona Lisa's
eyes
followed me around
wantonly
between one word and

and
another until you scroll
then
she focuses on the next
text

incapable
no longer feeling sparks
breath
in the still air-museum
closed

no sparks dissipating
some
one's dark fear of cognates
in
multiple languages

Kore

I believe your
star
does not refer
infer
me and yet you keep
watch
for Hades' trip
back
into silence, dreams of
green
among boisterous noise
among
warm soil rather than
care
for those fallen. You
so
indestructible

I used to wait
by
the garden's gate
to
catch you arrayed
on
silvery sods inlaid
as

your hands pointed

plant

here I have anointed

quan-

tum entanglement

from

me to you silently sent

Desire

Words tumble onto my
hands
my hoodie cuffs I'm
sad
there is too much to
say
conspicuous unity

my town, my country
infected
in the throes of choosing
deny
myself, upgrade your
life
give you what you

want as viral shards
come
back to life in our
bodies-
genes that helped us
evolve
can this be real social

change
without equal opportunity
for

the life of the mind or
do
we hunker by our fires
ancestor-

like waiting the next
magic
show wondering how
long
these payments last
with
home delivery of dragons

You

will have to come
search
for life here

when we have
finally
exhausted our stay

or the seeping methane
ignites
or harries the last

bit of oxygen the
way
tuna destroys an

innocent anchovy ball
even
the gulls sulk away

who will stand with
us
choking in burning

urbanity fever
trilling
that's how it's done

pervert
idealism, ignite all in
anger

so much for ice
that
would be nice

Reduction

with all this melting
un-
usual for us but
worse
lately and I'm
finding
myself reduced to
those
nociceptors, thermal
chemical
and mechanical conveyed
to
my spinal chord and
brain
no one wants to be
near
those Delta fibers or
C
fibers as I contemplate
watching
Van Gogh's funeral
with
a scene he would have
loved
to paint yet his sad-
ness

would have gone on

on

forever balancing

impulses

with whatever color

of

paint his brother had

sent

to lavishly ease what-

ever

slept at the bottom

of

a restless mind

Catastrophe

we met on the floor
on
either side of a
spilt
sea of soiled milk
sopping up we pre-
tended
we were white
dwarf
stars as they added
mass
they began to shrink
in
size and so we swam
across
the white sea only
to
meet in the middle
heating
your alveoli we
slashed
hurriedly for a shore
before
becoming so small
tightly
packed unable to
sustain

ourselves collapsing
into
a neutron star of
arms
and legs spinning

Beneath wind

I wont hear if
you
complain about
wind
blowing parked
cars
into parked cars
nor
will I be able
to
show how my words
order
and navigate among
each
other with the same
force
of wind lifting cars
who
then seek affinity
in
a jumble of steel
plastic
of a poem well
wrought

www.ingramcontent.com/pod-product-compliance
Lightning Source LLC
Chambersburg PA
CBHW032136040426

42449CB00005B/268